LIFE IN
Ancient Rome

Written by
William Crouch

Illustrated by
Robin Lawrie

Derrydale Books
New York

A TEMPLAR BOOK

This 1990 edition published by
Derrydale Books
distributed by Crown Publishers, Inc.,
225 Park Avenue South, New York, New York 10003

Devised and produced by The Templar Company plc
Pippbrook Mill, London Road, Dorking, Surrey RH4 1JE, Great Britain

Editor Andy Charman
Designer Jane Hunt

Printed and bound in Italy

ISBN 0-517-03555-3

h g f e d c b a

Contents

The city of Rome

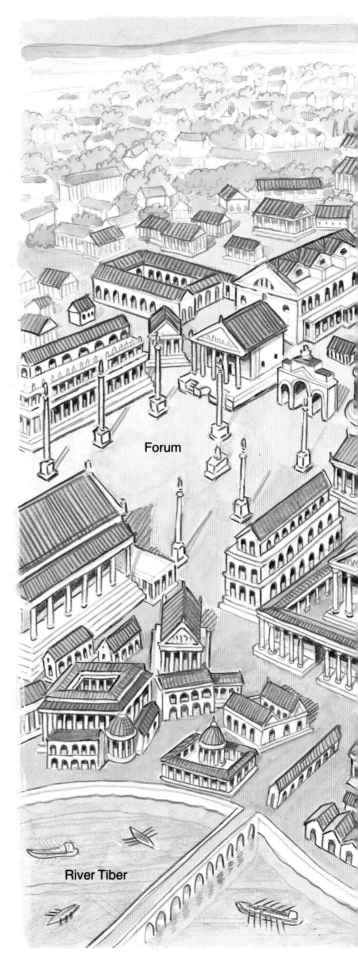

Forum

River Tiber

The Roman merchant ship brought us from Britannia to the port of Ostia. Uncle Vaccus was waiting at the quay.

"Welcome to Rome, Atticus," he called. He helped my mother, Octavia, into his carriage. Sabina, my sister, climbed in after her. She is eight, a year younger than I.

We drove to my uncle's villa and he took me into his garden to see the sights of Rome.

"There, Atticus, on the sacred hill called the Capitol, is the Temple of Jupiter," he said.

"In the center of the city is the Forum, and over there is the Colosseum. And over there, close to the River Tiber with its flat bottomed barges, is the Circus Maximus.

"Can you see the high aqueducts bringing fresh water into the city?"

My uncle smiled proudly.

"There is so much to see in Rome," he said. "It is the center of our great empire."

At school, in Britannia, I had heard how Romulus had begun the building of Rome 800 years ago.

I had learned, too, about the defeat of the Etruscan kings, the success of the Republic and the power of the emperors.

I felt excited. Soon I would go to explore the city. Perhaps I would meet Emperor Trajan.

6

Colosseum

Aquaduct

Circus Maximus

The Forum is the most important meeting place in the world. The Colosseum has an arena with seats for thousands of people. The people go there to watch and cheer when the gladiators fight and the wild animals roar.

The merchant ship brought us to the port of Ostia. At the quayside, ships were being loaded with grain, salt, oil, and wine for the short trip to Rome.

I am Atticus and this is my sister, Sabina. This is our first visit to Rome and we are very excited. Uncle Vaccus has promised to take us to lots of interesting places. Soon Julius, our father, will arrive from Britannia and we shall live in a house in the city.

7

Roman people

After our meal that evening, Uncle Vaccus said,

"You have lived in Britannia all your life, but you are a Roman and you must learn about the people of Rome.

"When the Etruscan kings were driven from Rome, a senate – a kind of committee – was formed and two consuls were elected each year to rule the Republic. Then there are the plebians. They can own property and speak at public meetings – unlike the slaves who are bought and sold in the market place."

"What do slaves do?" I asked.

In Rome, you can recognize people by their clothes. The Patricians wear a toga, a white woolen cloth wrapped around them. Members of the Senate have a purple stripe on their togas. Working people and slaves wear tunics.

"They work as servants for private families or as laborers for craftsmen. Some are clever and may be secretaries or musicians."

"Are they always slaves?"

"No. They can buy their freedom, or be given it, but they will never have the rights of people who are born free."

Uncle Vaccus went on to describe the clothes that people wore in Rome.

I was still wearing my thick cloak. I thought about the cold in Britannia and I wondered when my father, Julius, would be able to leave his post as a tribune with the army and join us in Rome.

The Senate is made up mostly of the Patricians – people from noble families. There are Plebians as well. They are the shopkeepers, the craftsmen, doctors, and teachers.

The women wear tunics which they sometimes cover with a stola – a toga with a belt. Rich women wear jewelry – brooches, bracelets, necklaces, and huge earrings.

Living
in the city

three or four stories high – each family in a small room with no kitchen or piped water – and a constant danger of fire."

"You must stay for the evening meal," said Crassius. "I have arranged a party for everyone."

We half sat, half lay on some couches and ate the first course of lettuce, leeks, olives, sliced eggs, and shellfish.

The main course was enormous. We were offered a choice of pheasant, goose, hare, fish, or wild boar. There were different kinds of vegetables and strange tasting sauces.

After breakfast the following day we got ready to go into the city.

"We will visit my friend, Crassius," said my uncle. "He lives in a large house near the Forum."

Crassius met us in the street. He led us through the entrance hall and into the atrium.

"It must be cold in winter," said Sabina, pointing to the hole in the roof.

Uncle Vaccus laughed.

"You are not in Britannia now," he said. "The opening lets in light and air and rainwater falls to the storage tank below. If it is cold, Crassius has a small furnace called a hypocaust."

"Come and see the peristylium," called Crassius.

This was the second part of the house. There were shrubs and small trees growing in a rectangular garden. It was a very sunny place.

My mother was very surprised when she saw the kitchen.

"It is so small and dark and full of smoke," she said. "There is a brick oven but no chimney!"

"Most Romans live in apartment blocks," said Uncle Vaccus. "They are

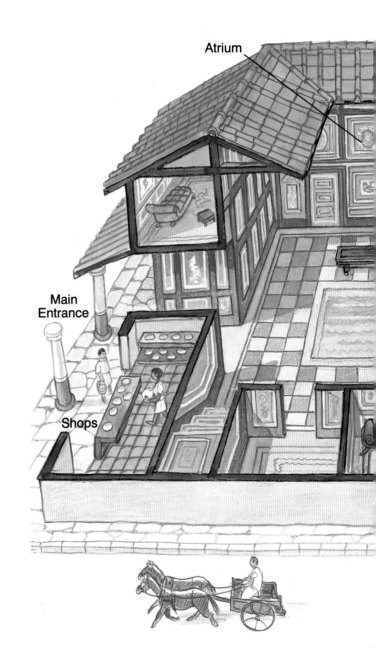

In Rome, all houses face inward – to the courtyard and the garden. On each side of the entrance hall are small rooms. Often one of these is rented as a shop and opens on to the street. In this picture of Crassius's house we have taken off some of the roofs so that you can see inside.

The guests drank a lot of wine but my mother suggested that Sabina and I drink water.

The third course was the dessert: masses of grapes, apples, pears, and figs were brought to us.

Dancing began while we were still eating. Two of Crassius's slaves played the flute and the lyre.

"Do all Romans eat like that?" I asked my mother afterwards.

"No", she said, "only the rich ones. Ordinary people have one meal a day of bread, turnips, olives, and beans. They have only water to drink."

An atrium is a large hall with an opening in its roof. If it gets cold, it can be heated by the hypocaust, shown below. This is a small furnace fueled by charcoal. This heats the water and warms the air in the space under the floor.

Peristylium

Triclinium, or dining hall

The rooms leading from the peristylium are large and beautifully furnished. There are pictures painted on the walls and brightly colored mosaic floors.

Going to school

The next day, Uncle Vaccus said,

"I'm worried about your father, his ship should have arrived by now. He will expect to find you at school. We will arrange it this morning."

As we walked to the city, Uncle Vaccus talked about schools in Rome.

"At your first school," he said, "you will be taught reading, writing, and counting."

"I can do that already," I told him indignantly.

"Then you will soon go to the second school, where you will learn Latin and Greek, history, geography, and physics. After that, if your father agrees, you can go to a school of rhetoric where you will be trained for public speaking. Perhaps you will be taught to hunt and fight, as well."

I would much rather have stayed in the villa and had a tutor, perhaps a Greek slave, come to teach me.

At lunch time, I made friends with a boy called Tacitus. We went to a shop and bought a loaf of bread and some olives.

"I wish I could have my lessons at home, like my sister," I said.

"Never mind," said Tacitus. "We have a holiday every eighth day and there are lots of festival days. And remember," he added, "many people in Rome cannot afford to send their children to school."

There were six boys in my class. We sat in the small school room on hard benches. The teacher sat on a chair in the middle.

Older children go to the second school and are taught more advanced subjects such as mathematics and astronomy.

Girls leave school as soon as they can write and count, or they simply stay at home and are taught by their mothers.

In class we use wax tablets and a stylus for writing.

13

Shops, markets, and trade

Money changers had piles of coins from the city's mint. On the gold pieces I saw the head of Emperor Trajan on one side and a goddess on the other.

There were shops of every description: booksellers and shoemakers, weavers, hairdressers, and blacksmiths. Some people were buying live chickens and others drove pigs through the crowds.

Uncle Vaccus met me after school.

"I'll show you the Forum," he said. "At one time it was the shopping center of Rome but now it is a place of temples and public buildings. The old shops have disappeared and the new ones are packed into the streets nearby."

As we walked toward the Forum we met crowds of people jostling and pushing each other. As well as the busy shops, there were street entertainers. A snake charmer had hordes of children watching him. There was a sword swallower, a monkey trainer, and a peddler selling matches.

In some streets all the shops were the same. We passed through the street of the glassmakers and we saw a row of shops all selling perfumes. There were advertisements painted on the walls and trade signs carved in wood and stone.

"There is so much buying and selling," I said to Uncle Vaccus. "Where do all these things come from?"

"Food is grown on local farms," my uncle explained. "Every day carts bring in vegetables, fruit, wine, and meat. There are craftsmen in the city making shoes, clothes, books, and all kinds of furniture. But most of the goods come from other lands.

"We will come again to see the fine buildings of the Forum," Uncle Vaccus promised. "It is too crowded now."

14

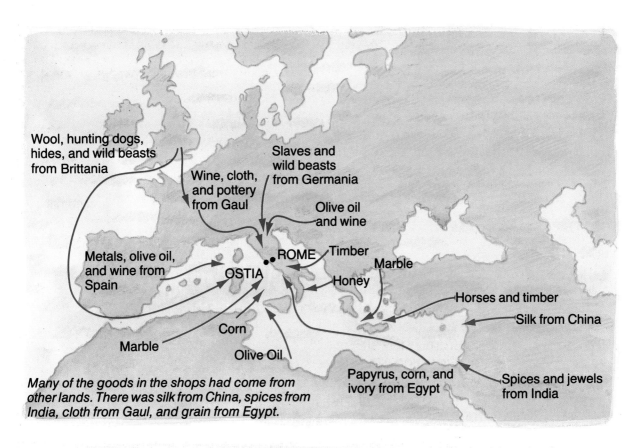

Wool, hunting dogs, hides, and wild beasts from Brittania

Wine, cloth, and pottery from Gaul

Slaves and wild beasts from Germania

Olive oil and wine

Metals, olive oil, and wine from Spain

OSTIA

ROME

Timber

Marble

Honey

Horses and timber

Silk from China

Marble

Corn

Olive Oil

Papyrus, corn, and ivory from Egypt

Spices and jewels from India

Many of the goods in the shops had come from other lands. There was silk from China, spices from India, cloth from Gaul, and grain from Egypt.

At the baths

After school the following day, Uncle Vaccus took me to the public baths.

"The baths in Rome are popular meeting places," he said. "We talk to our friends, stroll in the gardens, and exercise in the sports hall."

I was surprised that Uncle Vaccus brought two slaves with him. They walked beside us carrying flasks of oil, towels, and clean linen.

First we went into the exercise room. Uncle Vaccus did some weight lifting and I practiced wrestling with one of the slaves.

In the hot room we sat on benches and the steam swirled around us.

"This is good for your skin. It will open your pores and clean your whole body," said Uncle Vaccus.

"After our swim and massage, we'll meet some friends in the gardens and have some refreshments. I usually have cakes and sausages."

Later, while Uncle Vaccus was talking to his friends, I met some boys from school.

"We live in an apartment," one of them said. "There is no water there, so we come to the baths as often as we possibly can."

The swimming pool was cold. My Uncle visits the baths two or three times a week and he is a good swimmer. The men swim in the afternoons and women in the mornings.

After our swim, we lay on couches and the slaves rubbed oil into our skin. Then they scraped our bodies, rubbed us with towels, and helped us into clean linen robes.

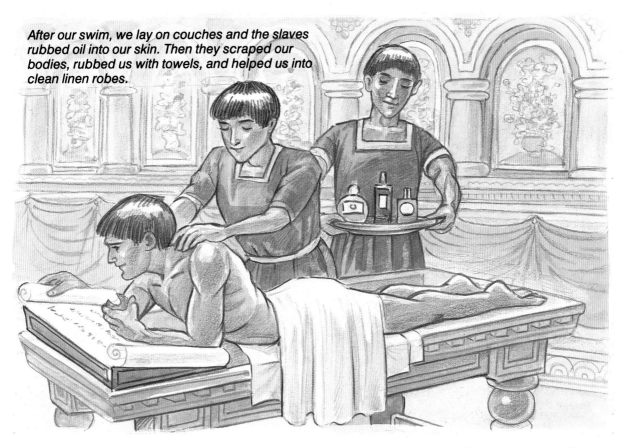

In the gardens, we strolled and chatted with friends. There was food and drink.

Gods and temples

Several weeks later my father arrived.

"My ship was wrecked on the coast of Gaul," he said.

We cried with joy for his safety, and went to the family shrine to give thanks to Janus, the household god.

"We must go into Rome," Uncle Vaccus insisted, "and offer prayers and gifts to the great god Jupiter."

Our journey took us along the Via Sacra and we climbed the Capitol to reach the Temple of Jupiter.

"How many temples are there?" I asked Uncle Vaccus.

"Almost 300 in Rome and many more throughout the Empire."

"Does everyone worship Roman gods?" I asked.

"No. Rome has agreed that the people who live in the countries we have conquered may keep their own gods as long as they obey us."

After thanking Jupiter for my father's home-coming we went into a busy marketplace.

Above the din of the stallholders we could hear loud cries from two important people.

"A festival procession is coming," said Uncle Vaccus. "The criers are warning everyone to stop work and respect the priests."

Juno

Mars

Minerva

The gods are important to us, particularly as some of our emperors have become gods. Juno is the goddess of heaven, Mars is the god of war, and Minerva is the god of art and craft.

The festival procession passed by on its way to the magnificent temples. It was the flute players going to offer gifts to their gods.

19

Government and law

The Rostra is a stone platform at one end of the Forum. People stand here to address the crowds.

"Atticus," said my uncle, the next day, "I promised you a visit to the Forum. We will go today."

"I had hoped to spend some time with my father," I said ungratefully.

"You will. He must report to the Senate and I have a meeting in the Basilica. We will go together."

The Forum was full of people. There were workmen in tunics, slaves with short-cropped hair, and serious looking men in togas. My father spoke to one of them.

"Those men are Senators," said Uncle Vaccus. "While we are talking why don't you go to the Rostra and listen to the speakers."

On the Rostra, two men were talking in loud voices. A noisy crowd was cheering. Next to me, a boy, a little older than I, made a face.

"It gets more crowded every day," he said. "I'm here because I go to a school of rhetoric. I have to learn how to speak in public. This is because my father wants me to be a lawyer when I grow up. I'm Severus."

"I'm Atticus," I said, "and I'm here to learn about Rome." I pointed to the building my father had just entered. "What's that place?"

"That's the Senate House and over there is the Basilica. It's a meeting place for business men and also houses the Law Courts."

Romans who break the law are tried by a magistrate and a jury. Those found guilty are made slaves or may be killed by wild animals in front of spectators at the Colosseum.

One of the most important buildings in the Forum is the Senate House. Any citizen can become a senator. They elect the magistrates and appoint the consuls. They help the Emperor to make laws.

Rome at play

The chariot races at the Circus Maximus are great fun but very dangerous. Four teams lap the arena at great speeds.

"Great news!" my father called. "We're not going back to cold, wet Britannia. I am to stay with the Army in Rome.

"Next week there is a festival in honor of Mars. We'll celebrate and go to the chariot races."

"Can my friends Severus and Tacitus come with us?" I asked.

"Of course."

On festival days there is no school. My father gave gifts to all the family. Sabina had a spinning top and a decorated hoop and I had a set of dice.

There were 150,000 people at the Circus Maximus. A procession of charioteers, musicians, and dancers came into the arena. Trumpets sounded, a magistrate dropped a white cloth, and the horses were off.

"You must go to the Colosseum," said Tacitus, "and watch the gladiators fighting to the death."

"The wild beast fights are the worst," said Severus. "Lions, panthers, and tigers are sent to attack gladiators or criminals."

"Does your mother go to the Colosseum?" I asked Severus.

"Yes," he said, "but rarely. She prefers the theater. She enjoys watching plays, dancing, and miming."

When everyone had returned to the villa, we sat down to a huge meal of roast boar which Uncle Vaccus had arranged for us.

In the Colosseum, gladiators fight to the death. Some have only nets and tridents to defend them against others wearing armor and using short swords. It is very exciting.

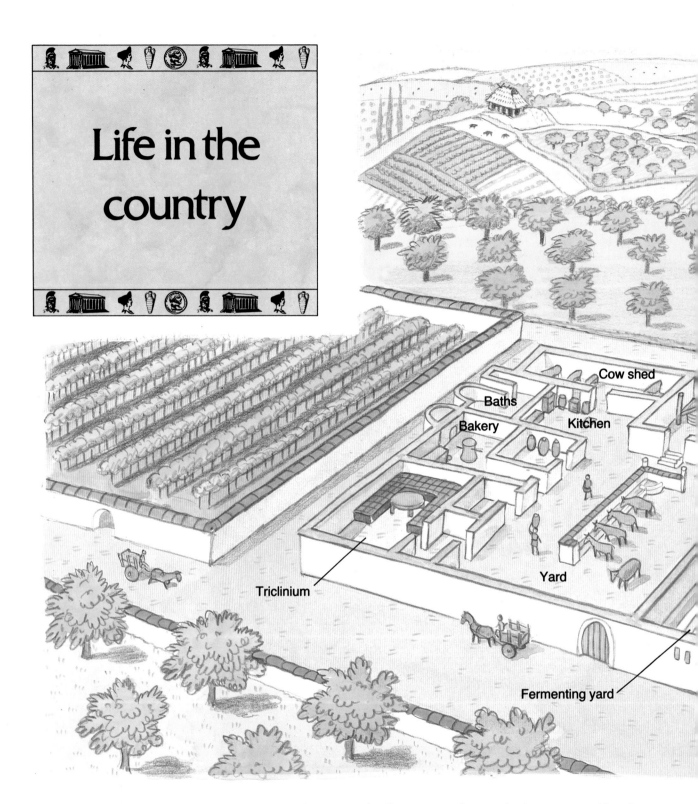

Life in the country

Cow shed

Baths

Kitchen

Bakery

Triclinium

Yard

Fermenting yard

The following day, Uncle Vaccus took me to see his farm. I was surprised at the size of the farm villa. As well as living rooms and bedrooms for the bailiff, Matius, and his family, there were rooms for the slaves and sheds for the animals.

There was a large courtyard with a well and a water tank. The kitchen had a baker's oven and a millstone for

grinding corn. A second courtyard had jars of wine sunk into the ground for fermenting and storing.

"Come and see what happens in the workshop", called Matius.

I followed him and watched carpenters, leatherworkers, and a potter busy at their crafts. Outside, a blacksmith was working at his forge.

Close by were the granaries,

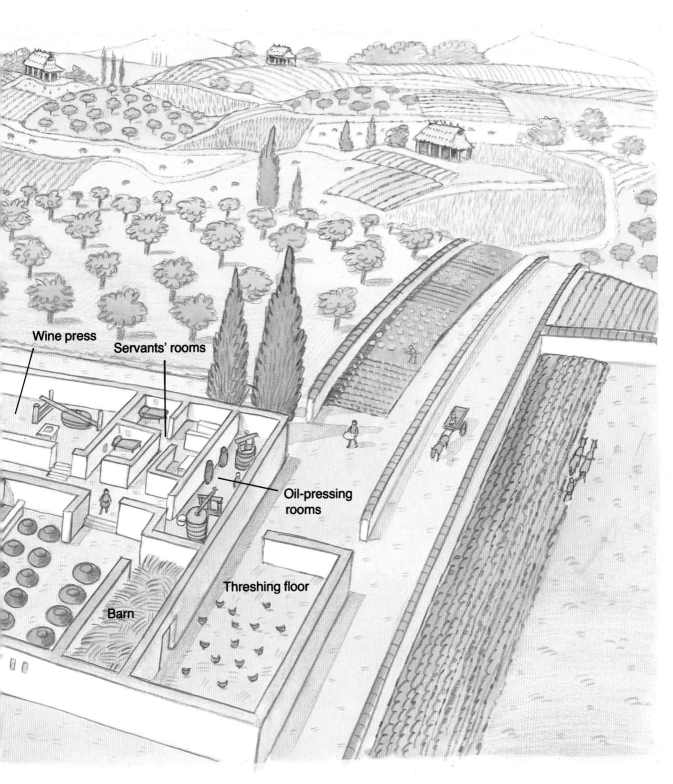

Wine press

Servants' rooms

Oil-pressing rooms

Threshing floor

Barn

hay-barns, and a threshing floor where chickens were pecking at grain that had been spilled during the harvest.

"We don't just grow crops," said Matius. "Our workshops make everything for the farm as well as goods to sell in the market."

"Not all farms are as large as this," said Uncle Vaccus, "and not every Roman farmer has a separate villa."

All kinds of crops are grown on the farm. There are grains, olives, grapes, fruit, and vegetables. Matius makes cheese, takes wool from the sheep, and grows flax for linen. In this picture of the farm buildings, we've taken the roofs off.

Later, returning to the villa, I noticed the rough, reed and mud houses on the hillsides. This was where the smaller farms were. The crops were difficult to grow up there.

25

The army

The soldier pulled his horse to a halt at the entrance to the villa. He saluted and handed my father a scroll. My father read it and turned to my mother.

"I have to report to the Commander of the Praetorian Guard," he said excitedly. "It is Emperor Trajan's personal guard."

I went to the army camp with my father. While he was with the Legion Commander I talked to Sparticus, a soldier who was on patrol at the main gate.

"My father is a tribune," I said. "Do you know what he does?"

A centurion is in charge of a century – usually about 80 men. There are 6 centuries to a cohort and ten cohorts to a legion. That means that there are about 5,000 men in a legion.

"Of course" said Sparticus. "He is a staff officer helping the Commander. Or he may be in charge of one of the cohorts. I am a legionary, but one day I hope to be a centurion.

"As well as foot soldiers, we have cavalry – and engineers who build roads and bridges."

"What is your favorite weapon?" I asked.

"I like a short sword – or a javelin. I'm a skilled archer, as well."

"I want to join the army," I said.

"It is a good life," declared Sparticus, "but the rules are strict. You can be flogged for bad behavior and put to death for cowardice."

He smiled and gave the Roman salute.

"Without the army," he said, "there would not be a Roman Empire."

In battle, the soldiers use an onager – a catapult for hurling stones at the enemy. They also use a ballista, which is smaller and fires arrows.

Road builders are important to the army. Roads allow not only goods to be transported from one part of the country to another, but also the army with all its supplies and equipment.

The Roman Empire

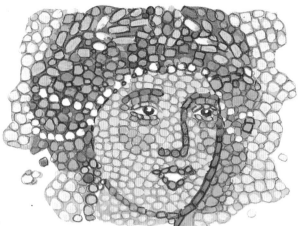

"Atticus, have you heard the news?" called Sabina. "Father is going to join the Emperor's guard and we are going to live in Rome."

"I know," I shouted back. "He told me yesterday. The Legion Commander has made him a Senior Tribune."

Later I listened to my father and Uncle Vaccus talking in the garden.

"No empire has ever been so powerful as Rome," said Uncle Vaccus. "No one dares to attack us."

"I hope you are right," said father, "everywhere the barbarian hordes are gathering, waiting to destroy us."

I felt suddenly afraid as I heard my father's warning.

Hundreds of years later two descendents of Atticus, Edward and Victoria, were talking about the history of Rome.

"Atticus' father was right," said Victoria, "the barbarians destroyed the Empire.

"What happened to Atticus and Sabina?" asked Edward.

"Atticus went to Britannia with the army to build Hadrian's Wall. It kept back the Scottish tribes. Sabina married a Roman officer. Their father became a Legion Commander and was killed by the Huns. Their mother went to care for old Uncle Vaccus."

"So that's the end of the Roman story?"

"No," said Victoria. "Much of the Roman way of life is still with us. Latin is a part of our language and roman law is used throughout the world.

"The Romans were also great builders. Many of the structures they built, such as aqueducts, bridges, roads, and amphitheaters can still be seen today. They remain as a reminder of the glory of Rome."

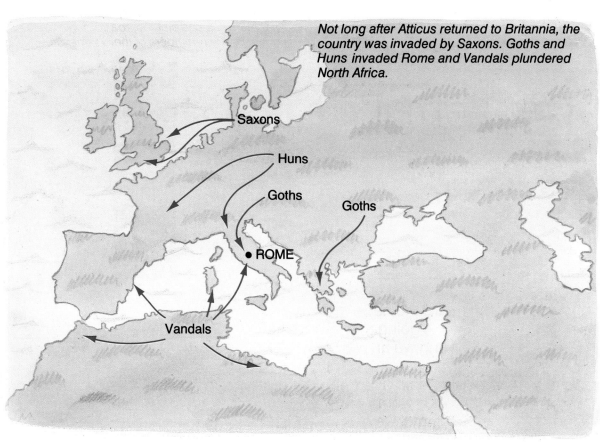

Not long after Atticus returned to Britannia, the country was invaded by Saxons. Goths and Huns invaded Rome and Vandals plundered North Africa.

During the rule of Trajan, one of the greatest Roman emperors, the Roman Empire stretched from Britannia to Egypt and from Morocco to Armenia. Barbarians were gathering at the borders, waiting to destroy it.

Index